WILDSAM

"The world was peopled
with wonders."

The origin of Wildsam comes from above, a
line of prose in the novel *East of Eden*, written by
John Steinbeck. Six words hinting at a broad and
interwoven idea. One of curiosity, connection, joy. And
the belief that stories have the power to unearth the
mysteries of a place—for anyone. The book in
your hands is rooted in such things.

WILDSAM

This book would not exist without the many people who warmly welcomed us into the Telluride community and the wider world of the San Juans. For insight and introductions, we thank Erik Dalton, J.T. Thomas, Paul Lucas, Kathryn Everett, Gabe Lifton-Zoline, Michael Gregory, Craig Childs, Sarah Lavender Smith and Amy Levek. We're grateful for the help and advice of Kate Jones of Telluride Arts, Shae LaPlace of Mountainfilm, Jennifer and Brad Ball of Between the Covers, and Alison Farnham of the Wilkinson Public Library. Next round of Flatliners is on us.

WILDSAM FIELD GUIDES™

Copyright © 2023

All rights reserved. No portion of this
book may be reproduced in any form without
permission from the publisher.

Published in the United States
by Wildsam Field Guides, Austin, Texas.

ISBN 978-1-4671-9990-2

Illustrations by Abigail Fox

To find more field guides, please visit
www.wildsam.com

CONTENTS

*Discover the people and places
that tell the story of Telluride*

ESSENTIALS 008

Trusted intel and travel info about iconic
places and important topics

BESTS 015

Selected recommendations for the most
authentic Telluride experiences

ALMANAC 023

Archival excerpts, timelines, clippings
and other historical musings

MAPS 043

Illustrated renderings of subject matter
vital to the town's heart and soul

INTERVIEWS 057

Concise and meaningful one-way conversations
with locals of note

STORIES 073

Essays and poems exploring the town and its
surroundings from respected Telluride writers

INDEX 093

NOTES 096

WELCOME

YOU DON'T END UP IN TELLURIDE by accident. Far from big cities and major airports, nestled into a box canyon surrounded by shimmering peaks, this town is out of the way no matter which way you're going. It is a dead-end town, in a literal sense. But those who have found their way here will assure you: It couldn't be more alive.

That wasn't always the case. By the 1960s, the mines that had once put the town on the map had nearly all closed. The Ghost Town Club of Colorado had even added Telluride to its roster of bygone settlements. Then, across 1972 through 1974, big moves began a reanimation: The first Telluride Film Festival, the first Telluride Bluegrass Festival. The opening of the Telluride Toggery and Between the Covers Bookstore on Colorado Avenue. And in the local election in the spring of 1974, a slate of long-haired skiers [or hippies, depending on whom you ask] swept the town council. Call it a revival: an ailing mining town reinvented as an adventurous, freewheeling, creative community.

Since then, more and more people from around the world have made their way to Telluride, drawn by its beauty and the vibrant culture that keeps thrumming thanks to that community's continued devotion. In winter come skiers; in summer, festival-goers, paying homage to mushrooms and jazz, film and, of course, bluegrass. No longer a few acts picking tunes on a rickety stage, Bluegrass is now a massive production and a premiere event of the genre, drawing thousands. Its success mirrors Telluride's growth and magnifies challenges: how to keep homes affordable and protect the lands and resources that make life here possible and pleasurable. The people of Telluride have weathered it all with a healthy mix of humor and chagrin—and the scrappy knack for innovation that life in an isolated mountain town requires.

Between the Covers is still here, though it recently moved a few doors down, into a bigger space with warm brick walls—once a Conoco garage, horse stables before that. The original bookstore is now an art space. The floorboards reveals well-worn paths: the grooves of decades of ski boots around phantom bookshelves. In that sense, maybe Telluride is a ghost town, in a good way. The past leaves traces, reminders of the journey to now. —The Editors

ESSENTIALS

LANDMARKS

Sheridan Opera House
Built in 1913 as a vaudeville theater, now a music venue. Considered Telluride's "living room" and architectural crown jewel.

Bridal Veil Falls
State's tallest free-falling cascade, at the head of the box canyon. Admire it from town, or hike for a close-up.

The Gondola
Free lift connecting Telluride to Mountain Village, with epic views. The "G" transports some 2.8 million passengers a year.

GREENSPACE

Town Park
Storied spot for music festivals, camping, rec leagues and disc golf. Wintertime: two skating rinks and a Nordic ski trail.

MEDIA

RADIO
KOTO
Community station since 1975. Listen to weekly *Off the Record* for thoughtful local debate.

MAGAZINE
Telluride Magazine
Locally owned mag, where news and literature mix.

ITINERARY

Morning. Breakfast at The Butcher & The Baker. Book-browsing at Between the Covers. Coffee and a treat from Bruno.
Midday. The mountains call. Depending on season and ambition: hit the slopes, ice skate at Town Park, hike up to Bridal Veil Falls or head out to Alta Lakes for paddleboarding.
Evening. Wander Colorado Ave, popping into Slate Gray Gallery and MiXX to see some local and regional art. Dinner at The National, nightcap at There.

FOODWAY

Breakfast burrito
The perfect pre-adventure meal comes tucked into a snug tortilla blanket, steaming and full of goodness. Blessedly found all around, from gas stations to gourmet cafes, but The Butcher & The Baker's iteration is a local favorite: fresh farm eggs, melty cheddar, salsa, corn, black beans, sweet potatoes. Add sausage for extra oomph.

MUSEUM

Telluride Historical Museum
Built as a hospital in 1896. Its 10 rooms now span artifacts and exploration of Ute heritage, mining, skiing and festival history.

LODGING

New Sheridan Hotel
Historic spot in the heart of town. People-watch at the carved mahogany Parlor bar.

Dunton Town House
19th-century inn built by Trentino-Tyrolean immigrants and miners. Renovated with those roots in mind by the folks behind Dunton Hot Springs.

The Bivvi Hostel Telluride
Cozy, affordable option with open-mic nights and a restaurant.

Madeline Hotel & Residences
Classy Mountain Village resort with local touches [see: leather menus from Crossbow]. Fly-fish, ride horses or fly to Moab.

The Peaks Resort & Spa
Choose luxury suite or log cabin. The biggest draw: an unforgettable two-story water slide.

Lumière with Inspirato
Boutique ski-in at the base of Lift 4. Soak in the hot tub after a day on the slopes.

CULTURE

BOOKS

▷ *Telluride Bluegrass Festival: Forty Years of Festivation* by Dan Sadowsky: Published in 2014, a celebration of the festival's past and present.

▷ *Tomboy Bride* by Harriet Fish Backus: One woman's firsthand account of the pioneer days, when Telluride was a rowdy mining town.

MUSIC

▷ *Telluride Sessions* by Strength in Numbers: Bluegrass supergroup: Sam Bush, Jerry Douglas, Béla Fleck, Mark O'Connor, Edgar Meyer:

▷ *American Siren* by Emily Scott Robinson: Local singer-songwriter describes her own work as "halfway between country and folk."

FILM

▷ *The YX Factor*: 2004 documentary explores the unique community forged in 1970s Telluride with the advent of the ski resort.

▷ *True Grit*: Many scenes from the 1969 original, starring John Wayne in his only Academy Award-winning role, were filmed in the San Juans.

HISTORY

1875 .... First placer and lode claims in the San Miguel Mining District
1878 .... Town of Columbia incorporated
1881 .... Ute peoples forced to leave the area, part of their ancestral territory
1887 .... Columbia is renamed Telluride
1889 .... Butch Cassidy's first bank robbery: San Miguel Valley Bank
1890 .... Rio Grande Southern Railroad crosses Dallas Divide
1891 .... World's first long-distance transmission of alternating-current electricity achieved in nearby Ames, CO
1893 .... Silver market crashes, hampering mining endeavors
1896 .... Hall's Hospital is built, operates until 1964
1901 .... Western Federation of Miners Union Local No. 63 goes on strike, part of violent and complicated "Colorado Labor Wars"
1902 .... Presidential candidate William Jennings Bryan makes famed "Cross of Gold" speech at New Sheridan Hotel
 .... An avalanche kills 16 and damages buildings at Liberty Bell Mine
1914 ... Summer storm swells Cornet Creek; flood causes extensive damage
1918 .... Mining enters a depressed era, due partly to flu epidemic and end of World War I-driven demand
1931 .... First Galloping Goose "railbus" built, traverses San Juan Mountains
1962 .... Downtown Telluride designated a National Historic Landmark
1972 .... California entrepreneur Joseph Zoline founds Telluride Ski Resort
1973 .... Unofficial Telluride Bluegrass debut: about 1,000 people festivate
1974 .... First Telluride Film Festival
1975 .... Béla Fleck performs at Telluride Bluegrass, beginning run of 45 consecutive years
1977 .... Telluride Jazz Festival joins the cultural roster
1979 .... Mountainfilm founded
1978 .... Telluride's last remaining mines close
1981 .... First Telluride Mushroom Festival
1987 .... Grateful Dead plays two legendary shows at Town Park
1996 .... Gondola begins running between Telluride and Mountain Village
2003 .... Ski area expansion to encompass Prospect Bowl
2007 ... Valley Floor Preservation Partners and Town of Telluride raise $50 million to purchase the Telluride Valley Floor
2009 ... Town council approves a conservation easement to permanently protect the Valley Floor

ABOUT TOWN

ESTABLISHED 1878

ELEVATION
8,750 FEET

HISTORIC AREA
DOWNTOWN

GREAT WALK
SAN MIGUEL RIVER TRAIL

FESTIVAL
MOUNTAINFILM

CIVIC LIFE

LOCAL LIBRARY
Wilkinson Public Library
100 W Pacific Ave

HOMEGROWN HERO
Bobby Brown
Winter X Games gold winner

SPORTING CLUB
Telluride Lizard Heads
telluridehockey.com

HISTORIC GRAVEYARD
Lone Tree Cemetery
Mining-boom era

SERVICES

TRAIL INFO
Telluride Mountain Club
telluridemountainclub.org

FREE BUS
Galloping Goose
Loops through town

SKI BOOT FITTING
Bootdoctors
236 S Oak St

BIKE RENTAL
Easy Rider
124 E Pacific Ave

NAVIGATION

Tucked into a box canyon in the rugged San Juan Mountains, Telluride is out of the way—that's part of its charm. Unless you fly into the small local airport, getting here requires traversing mountain passes and hairpin turns, so drive with care. The town of Telluride lies down in the valley. Mountain Village, home of Telluride Ski Resort, is a whole separate town to the southwest, higher than Telluride at 9,600 feet. A free gondola connects the two.

SELECTED CONTENT

016–017 *Food & Drink*

BREAKFAST
APRÈS
PIZZA
SMALL PLATES

018 *Shopping*

BOOKS
CUSTOM SKIS
LEATHER GOODS
WINE

019 *Action*

SNOWMOBILE TOUR
CLIMBING
HOT SPRINGS
LOCAL PERFORMANCE

020 *Festivals & Events*

MOUNTAINFILM
BLUEGRASS
RODEO
ART WALK

021 *Experts*

SCIENCE RESEARCH
CERAMICS
ADAPTIVE SPORTS
METALWORK

MORE THAN 70 PICKS ↪

BESTS

A curated list of town favorites—classic and new—from bars and restaurants to shops and experiences, plus a handful of can't-miss experts

BESTS

FOOD & DRINK

BREAKFAST

The Butcher & The Baker
201 E Colorado Ave
Telluride
Handmade breads, farm-fresh eggs. Day Maker sandwich fulfills its promise.

....

BARBECUE

Oak
250 W San Juan Ave
Telluride
Smoking briskets for 25 years. Can't go wrong with fried okra and the po'boy of the day.

....

SUNSET SPOT

Allred's
San Sophia Station
Mid-gondola
Snag bar seats by the window for prime alpenglow with drinks and apps.

APRÈS

Gorrono Ranch
565 Mountain Village Blvd, Mtn Village
Piping beef chili, right on the mountain. Lounge with cocktails on the "snow beach."

....

DATE NIGHT

The National
100 E Colorado Ave
Telluride
Exposed brick, artful dishes. Always save room for coconut cream pie.

....

NEW AMERICAN

221 South Oak
221 S Oak St
Telluride
Unique takes on Rocky Mountain flavors from *Top Chef* finalist Eliza Gavin. Full veg menu too.

SLOPESIDE DINNER

Alpino Vino
12100 Camels' Garden Rd
Mountain Village
Ski in or take a heated snowcoach. Winter only.

....

STEAKHOUSE

New Sheridan Chop House
231 W Colorado Ave
Telluride
Get your steak "Oscar Style": topped with béarnaise and blue lump crab.

....

HAPPY HOUR

Cosmopolitan
301 Gus's Way
Telluride
At the base of the gondola, Chef Chad Scothorn serves up eclectic fare, seared duck to sushi.

MODERN CHALET
La Marmotte
150 W San Juan Ave
Telluride
French fare and fine wine in a sweetly rustic cabin.

....

MEXICAN
La Cocina de Luz
123 E Colorado Ave
Telluride
Enchiladas and chilaquiles: low-key, locally sourced.

....

ITALIAN
Rustico
114 E Colorado Ave
Telluride
Come for the hearty pastas; stay for the endless wine list.

....

THAI
Siam
200 S Davis St
Telluride
Dishes hum with complex flavor and balanced spice.

....

PIZZA
Brown Dog Pizza
110 E Colorado Ave
Telluride
Detroit-style square pies are the go-to. Down-to-earth sports bar vibes.

ON-MOUNTAIN LUNCH
Bon Vivant
Telluride Ski Resort
Mountain Village
Crepes and charcuterie on the deck, atop Lift 5. Winter only.

....

MIDDLE EASTERN
Caravan
123 E Colorado Ave
Telluride
Trailer serving top-notch falafel and fresh smoothies.

....

BURGER
Floradora Saloon
103 W Colorado Ave
Telluride
The place to rehash wipeout stories over beers after a long ski [or hike] day.

....

BRASSERIE
Petite Maison
219 W Pacific Ave
Telluride
Parisian parlor, mountain charm.

....

SMALL PLATES
Timber Room
568 Mountain Village Blvd, Mtn Village
Cozy up to the fire pit for champagne, "Devilish Eggs" and fondue savoyarde.

COCKTAILS
There
627 W Pacific Ave
Telluride
Tucked-away spot, perfect Manhattans.

....

OLD-SCHOOL BAR
New Sheridan Parlor
231 W Colorado Ave
Telluride
Sip a Flatliner, Telluride's espresso martini-esque signature drink.

....

TAPROOM
Telluride Brewing Company
156 Society Dr
Lawson Hill
Some of the state's best IPAs.

....

BREW PUB
Smuggler Union
225 S Pine St
Telluride
Try the lauded Blonde Betty, brewed with coriander.

....

BRATS & BEER
Stronghouse
283 S Fir St
Telluride
Traditional or elk jalapeño. With a German lager, please.

SHOPS

BOOKS
Between the Covers
214 W Colorado Ave
Telluride
Slinging literature, lodge reads and guidebooks since 1974. [Now in a bigger space.]

....

SKIS
Wagner Custom Skis
620 Mountain Village Blvd, Mtn Village
Where science meets skiing to make art.

....

CLOTHING
Telluride Toggery
109 E Colorado Ave
Telluride
Telluride's oldest store. Boots, denim and sundresses.

....

HARDWARE
Timberline Ace Hardware
200 E Colorado Ave
Telluride
If they don't have it, you don't need it. And if you don't see it, just ask Tom.

OUTDOOR GEAR
Jagged Edge Mountain Gear
223 E Colorado Ave
Telluride
Local line of packs and clothes alongside other quality brands. Drop in for demos.

....

INSTRUMENTS
Telluride Music Co.
333 W Colorado Ave
Telluride
Stringed selection fit for a bluegrass town. Acoustic and electric guitars, mandolins.

....

FLOWERS
Flowers By Ella
359 E Colorado Ave
Telluride
Gorgeous arrangements inspired by local landscapes.

....

WINE
Telluride Bottle Works
129 W San Juan Ave
Telluride
Wide selection, hard-to-find bottles.

LEATHER GOODS
Crossbow
101 W Colorado Ave
Telluride
Custom hat bar, stylish western wear. Owned by two local women.

....

FISHING GEAR
Telluride Angler
221 W Colorado Ave
Telluride
Rods, reels and guided trips to the San Miguel and beyond.

....

SWEETS
Telluride Truffle
171 S Pine St
Telluride
Mountain-shaped truffles for mountain-minded people.

....

PICNIC
Over the Moon
223 S Pine St
Telluride
Beautiful charcuterie and cheese plates, fancy pantry goods and gifts.

ACTION

SNOWMOBILE TOUR

Telluride Outfitters
tellurideoutfitters.com
Cruise out to Alta Lakes Ghost Town or all the way to Dunton Hot Springs [soak included].

....

CLIMBING

Telluride Mountain Guides
telluridemountainguiding.com
Options abound year-round. Target Ames Falls for ice, Pipeline Wall for rock.

....

PADDLEBOARD

Alta Lakes
South of Telluride
Crystal-clear calm waters with dispersed camping nearby.

....

HOT SPRINGS

Orvis Hot Springs
1585 County Rd 3
Ridgway
Several soothing pools of natural lithium water. Clothing optional.

IN-TOWN HIKE

Jud Wiebe Trail
North end of Aspen St
One of the first trails to shed its snow. Snowshoe-able too. 2.7 miles round trip; epic mountain views.

....

GOLF

Telluride Ski & Golf Club
thepeaksresort.com
Tee off surrounded by San Juan peaks at one of the highest courses anywhere.

....

LOCAL PERFORMANCE

The Fig
@thefigtelluride
Arts pop-ups span comedy nights, spoken-word and more. Check out their zine too.

....

HISTORY TOUR

Ashley Boling
telluridemuseum.org
Local raconteur knows Telluride's history and architecture inside and out.

SKI SCHOOL

Telluride Ski Resort
lessons@telski.com
Explore groomed and ungroomed terrain in private or small-group lessons, half-day or full.

....

4WD TOUR

Telluride Outside
tellurideoutside.com
Get your high-country thrills on a ride to historic Tomboy Ghost Town.

....

BIG HIKE

Sneffels Highline Trail
North end of Aspen St
This 13-mile loop traverses aspen forest and alpine basins. Waterfalls, streams wildflowered slopes.

....

NORDIC SKIING

Telluride Nordic Association
telluridenordic.com
Maintains seven local trail systems, including Trout Lake.

FESTIVALS & EVENTS

DOCUMENTARY
Mountainfilm
mountainfilm.org
May
Showcasing short films on the outdoors since 1979.

....

BLUEGRASS
Telluride Bluegrass Festival
bluegrass.com/telluride
June
Soulful twang under the stars. Book extra early for camping.

....

RODEO
San Miguel Basin Rodeo
@sanmiguel basinrodeo, July
Pull on your boots for mutton busting and other classics.

....

JAZZ
Telluride Jazz Festival
telluridejazz.org
August
Don't miss the rollicking New Orleans Second Line parade.

FUNGI
Mushroom Festival
tellurideinstitute.org
August
A mycological celebration, from cultivation to psychedelic research.

....

MUSIC & BEER
Blues & Brews Festival
tellurideblues.com
September
Microbrews pair well with blues [also funk, gospel, soul].

....

CINEMA
Telluride Film Festival
telluridefilm festival.org, September
Launched *Juno*, *Brokeback Mountain*, and more.

....

IDEAS
Original Thinkers Festival
originalthinkers.com
October
Fresh dialogue on navigating our world.

BENEFIT
Telluride AIDS Benefit Fashion Show
tellurideaids benefit.org, February
Wearable art for good since 1994.

....

LGBTQ+
Telluride Gay Ski Week
telluridegayski.com
February
An inclusive celebration on the slopes.

....

ART
First Thursday Art Walk
telluridearts.org
Monthly
Curated meander through local galleries, with snacks and drinks.

....

CULINARY CULTURE
Telluride Food & Vine
telluridefoodandvine. com, June
Vino, Cocktails, feasts-and balloons.

EXPERTS

PHOTOGRAPHY
Ryan Bonneau
@ryanbonneauphoto
Talented capturer of local landscapes. No wonder he shoots for the tourism board.

SCIENCE RESEARCH
Mark Kozak
telluridescience.org
With a background steeped in snow physics, runs eco-focused Telluride Science & Innovation Center.

BLUEGRASS FESTIVAL
Tom Heidger
telluridetom.com
To festivarians, he's known as Telluride Tom. Awarded a lifetime festival pass and named mayor of Town Park in 2003.

RESTAURATEUR
Josh Klein
smugglerunion.com
New Orleans-raised chef behind Smuggler Union and other local spots.

SKIING
Gus Kenworthy
@guskenworthy
Telluride-raised. Won a silver for the U.S. in the 2014 Olympics. A dual citizen, he now competes for Britain.

CONSERVATION
Mason Osgood
sheepmountain alliance.org
Mayor of Ophir, Sheep Mountain Alliance director.

CERAMICS
Tara Carter
@youpinchityoupotit
Pinches beautiful, swirly pots. Manages Wheel House pottery co-operative.

ADAPTIVE SPORTS
Telluride Adaptive Sports Program
telluride adaptivesports.org
Veterans' climbing, backcountry handcycling, adaptive skiing and SUP.

TRAILS
Heidi Lauterbach
telluride mountainclub.org
Directs Telluride Mountain Club, which maintains trails. Dog named Annie Oakley.

METALWORK
Jeff Skoloda
skolstudio.com
Projects include Ouray Ice Festival trophies, like an eagle made of welded ice-climbing picks.

COMMUNITY ADVOCACY
Ximena Rebolledo Léon
Telluride Regional Medical Center
Nurse prioritizes outreach to Latino community.

POET LAUREATE
Joanna Spindler
@joannaspindrift
Librarian, climber and all-around bright spark.

SELECTED CONTENT

- 024 *Ghosts & Edward Abbey*
- 025 *Wildflowers*
- 026 *Hardrock 100*
- 027 *Vladimir Nabokov*
- 029 *Ski History*
- 031 *Historic Buildings*
- 032 *Gold King Mine*
- 033 *1976 Drug Bust*
- 034 *Butch Cassidy*
- 035 *Nothing Festival*
- 036 *The Grateful Dead*
- 037 *Galloping Goose*
- 039 *Great Flood & Ute History*
- 041 *Alpine Lakes*

ALMANAC

*A deep dive into the cultural heritage of
Telluride through news clippings, timelines
and other historical hearsay*

ALMANAC

HAUNTINGS

THE SILVER BELL

This was once an infamous brothel. By the time the building was restored in the 1980s, much of it hadn't been disturbed in 100 years. In 1986, builders were working on the building when they heard something that raised goosebumps on their arms: the hollow sound of a woman's wavering, anguished voice. They froze. The house was empty. But day after day, the voice came back. Shreds of a piano tune rippled through the house. Yellow roses appeared. Then, one morning, workers encountered a photo on the floor. It depicted a prostitute named Ramona. Her fate remains unknown, but the photo was carefully removed. The voice never returned.

TELLURIDE HISTORICAL MUSEUM

Around 2002, the museum began having problems with an ancient X-ray machine that was part of its historical exhibits. It kept flickering on at night, accompanied by blaring alarms. Neither security nor electricians could supply an explanation. But a paranormal investigator pointed to the building's origins as a hospital during the town's mining boom. Then, miners lived in fear of consumption, the common name for a variety of deadly mining-related lung diseases. A positive X-ray was a career-ender. Desperate, the museum held a ceremony, assuring the spirits that the new X-ray exhibit was for education—not to "out" anyone. Immediately after, the mysterious activity stopped.

EDWARD ABBEY

In an October 1976 cover story for *High Country News*, Edward Abbey, author of *Desert Solitaire* and *The Monkey Wrench Gang*, turned his trademark sardonic wit and crotchety gaze to Telluride. The headline: "Telluride Blues, a Hatchet Job." "Telluride was actually discovered back in 1957, by me, during a picnic expedition into the San Miguel Mountains of southwestern Colorado," he quipped. "I recognized it at once as something much too good for the general public." He kept the place a secret from all except his "closest picnicking cronies." But it was no use, he lamented: "I should have invested everything I had in Telluride real estate."

WILDFLOWERS OF NOTE

MULE'S EARS *Wyethia amplexicaulis* Montane plant spreads sunshine-yellow among the evergreens and wildlife tracks of the springtime Valley Floor. *When:* May to June *Where:* San Miguel Valley Floor

FIREWEED *Chamerion angustifolium* Literally sprouting from the ashes, this blushed flower thrives in scorched areas and forest openings, along roadsides and at the forest's edge. *When*: June to September *Where*: San Miguel River Trail

LITTLE RED ELEPHANT *Pedicularis groenlandica* Near streams and springs large colonies of incarnadine flowers bloom. The long, curvy upper lip evokes an elephant's trunk. *When*: June to August *Where*: Bridal Veil Falls Trail

SCARLET PAINTBRUSH *Castilleja coccinea* Flourishing from the foothills to the subalpine, scarlet paintbrush indeed paints Telluride's summertime canvas in strokes of red and orange. *When*: May to September *Where*: Wasatch Trail

KING'S CROWN *Rhodiola integrifolia* Sits atop the alpine zone, where its leafy stem can soar to 20 inches and its petals emulate the deep red of a full-bodied wine. *When*: June to August *Where*: Sneffels Highline Trail

COLORADO COLUMBINE *Aquilegia coerulea* The state flower ranges from the foothills to the high alpine. Its slender stem blossoms into five large lavender sepals that frame creamy white petals. *When*: June to August *Where*: Copper Mountain

SILVERY LUPINE *Lupinus argenteus* Reaching as high as 20 skinny inches, with a spike of cool blue and purple petals. Silvery lupine attracts butterflies to the roads, slopes and open wilderness it calls home. *When*: May to August *Where*: Last Dollar Road

BLUEBELL *Campanula rotundifolia* Delicate though it appears, the tall, dangling bluebell is hardy enough to withstand southwest Colorado's harsh high-alpine conditions. *When*: July to September *Where*: Along the roadside

MONKSHOOD *Aconitum columbianum* When monsoon season arrives in the depths of summer, it summons monkshood's aubergine blooms. A sultry flower found in wetlands. Poisonous: don't touch! *When*: June to September *Where*: Bear Creek Falls Trail

HARDROCK 100

In 1991, a ragtag handful of Colorado runners dreamed up an endurance race through the San Juan Mountains. Named in tribute to the grit of the state's hardrock miners, the route would connect iconic mining towns via old mine roads—no matter how steep or remote. The dreamers charted a course and announced the first race. Few showed up. Fewer finished. But the idea stuck: Today, the Hardrock 100 boasts one of the world's toughest—and most legendary—ultramarathon courses. Bears, elk and mountain lions wander the trails. Alpine thunderstorms strike daily. Breakdowns and hallucinations are common. Other key stats:

INAUGURAL RACERS
42 starters,
18 finishers

MODERN RACERS
2,200 annual applicants,
145 starters

MOUNTAIN PASSES
13

STREAM CROSSINGS
50+

CALORIES BURNED
up to 16,000

TOTAL RACE DISTANCE
102.5 miles

TOTAL ELEVATION CHANGE
66,394 feet

AVERAGE COURSE ELEVATION
11,000 feet

HIGHEST POINT
14,048 feet

CUT-OFF TIME
48 hours

FASTEST TIME (MEN
21:36:24
[Kilian Jornet]

FASTEST TIME (WOMEN)
26:44:36
[Courtney Dauwalter]

THE NAME OF TELLURIDE

Telluride was founded in 1878 as "Columbia" but renamed in 1887 to avoid confusion with a California town by the same name. The name "Telluride" came from gold telluride minerals—such as calaverite, krennerite and petzite—which contain the element tellurium. Though the town was a mining hub, and much gold and silver came out of the surrounding mines, no telluride minerals were ever actually found in the vicinity.

NABOKOV'S BUTTERFLY

In the summer of 1951, Vladimir Nabokov came to Telluride in search of females of the butterfly species that would become known as Lycaeides sublivens Nabokov. *Below, an excerpt from the celebrated novelist's report, originally published in* The Lepidopterists' News, *August 8, 1952.*

When reached at last, Telluride turned out to be a damp, unfrequented, but very spectacular cul-de-sac [which a prodigious rainbow straddled every evening] at the end of two converging roads, one from Placerville, the other from Dolores, both atrocious. There is one motel, the optimistic and excellent Valley View Court where my wife and I stayed, at 9,000 feet altitude, from the 3rd to the 29th of July, walking up daily to at least 12,000 feet along various more or less steep trails in search of *sublivens*. Once or twice Mr. Homer Reid of Telluride took us up in his jeep.... After 10 days of this, and despite diligent subsequent exploration, only one sparse colony of *sublivens* was found.... The colony I found was restricted to one very steep slope reaching from about 10,500 to a ridge at 11,000 feet and towering over Tomboy Road between "Social Tunnel" and "Bullion Mine."

THE FREE BOX

Walking along bustling Colorado Avenue, as you pass Pine Street, you'll likely notice what appears to be some kind of outdoor shop extending north up the block. In fact, nothing here is for sale; it's all free. This is the Telluride Free Box, a local tradition dating back to 1977. More a series of cubbies than an actual box, it's a place where locals and passers-through can give and take usable clothing, household items, books and more. In addition to meeting basic needs, come the end of ski season, the Free Box can be a great spot to nab lightly used gear. It's up to the community to keep the Free Box in good working order: rules about neatness, sorting and general goodwill ["The FREE BOX is a privilege, not a right, so let's all take care of it"] are painted on the wood.

A 1993 Patagonia catalog featured a photo of a baby in the Free Box—on, of course, the shelf labeled "BABIES." [Photographer and pro skier Gary Bigham took the photo of his daughter, Guri.]

SKI HISTORY

1878 .... Miners settle in Telluride

1937 .... William "Senior" Mahoney, other miners ski with towropes powered by gas engine

1959 .... Locals form Telluride Ski, Inc. and raise money for a ski area, but lack investors

1967 .... *Skiing Magazine* features Joern Gerdts' images of Telluride covered in snow

.... California lawyer Joseph T. Zoline buys land for a ski area in Telluride

1970 .... With lifts still under construction, skiers pay $12.50 a day for snowcat access, lunch

1972 .... Telluride Ski Resort opens with five lifts turning

1975 .... Installation of Lift 7 connects the town of Telluride to the ski area

1978 .... Idarado, the last mine in Telluride, closes

.... Coloradans Ron Allred and Jim Wells buy the ski area from Zoline

1981 .... After a dry season, a snowmaking system is installed

1985 .... Lifts 4, 8 [the original Lift 4] and 9 are built

1986 .... First high-speed lift installed

1987 .... The town of Mountain Village is established

1992 .... Development of Telluride Golf creates year-round appeal

1996 .... The Telluride Mountain Village Gondola opens

2000 .... Ski resort acquires 733-acre Prospect Bowl expansion

2001 .... Investor Hideo "Joe" Morita purchases Telluride Ski and Golf Resort

2004 .... Entrepreneur Chuck Horning acquires the resort

.... Double black diamond Mountain Quail opens to the public

2008 .... Palmyra Peak, Revelation Bowl and Gold Hill Chutes open to the public

.... Second-highest elevation restaurant in North America, Alpino Vino, opens

2012 .... Voted #1 in North America in *Condé Nast Traveler*'s Readers' Choice Awards, repeating in 2013, 2014

2018-19... Historic snowfall season: 318.8 inches

2022 .... Telluride Ski [a.k.a. Telski] celebrates 50 years

2023 .... First all-women ski patrol team runs Telluride Station

NEW SKI SLOPE PLANNED

Fort Lewis Independent,
October 22, 1971

Last Friday at the historic Sheridan Hotel in Telluride, two Use Permits were signed by Joseph T. Zoline and Art Martin to insure the development of a ski area in Telluride.

Zoline, the developer of the area, has stressed the fact that he is using comprehensive development planning to ensure preservation of the environment. The Use Permits were presented by Martin, Forest Supervisor of the Grand Mesa, Uncompahgre District, for Zoline to insure the use of 2,520 acres of forest land.

Both Martin and Zoline feel the area may become the best in the United States. Through the extensive geological, topographical and engineering data gathered by Zoline's staff many precautions will be taken to stress the protection of the environment. Already there is a real estate boom in San Miguel county, with extensive development planned for the future. Steps are already being taken to establish an airport in the county to handle the expected ski trade.

Another significant development will be the construction of a major highway into Telluride. It is expected that the road will follow the current route of the road from Cortez, through Dolores and Rico, to Telluride. Because of the future dam project at the Dallas divide, it is likely the road will not come in from Montrose and Ridgway.

On the other side of the fence there are many residents of San Miguel county who do not want to see the project begin. Some of these people feel that the historic value of Telluride and the surrounding area will be diminished because of the development and expansion. They point to Aspen and Vail as examples of the ski boom, and believe the proposed area in Telluride will also get out of hand. To this, Zoline says, "I intend to preserve the historic charm and character of Telluride, and I will continue to be opposed to anything or anyone who might destroy the environment."

Martin feels that the development has had comprehensive and thorough planning, and says that the Forest Service "has tried to provide full assistance in developing plans in complete harmony with the environment." Construction is expected to begin next summer on the chairlifts, while assistance from the Forest Service continues as Zoline develops and refines his plans.

HISTORIC BUILDINGS OF NOTE

Though Telluride's mining bust, which unfolded in the 1950s and '60s, was economically devastating, it inadvertently resulted in the salvation of the town's now-historic structures. With no money for demolition, most buildings were left untouched. The result is a living snapshot of the old Wild West.

TOWN HALL 1883
The oldest building in town. Built as a one-room schoolhouse, later repurposed for civic proceedings. *113 W Columbia Ave*

SAN MIGUEL COUNTY COURTHOUSE 1887
Telluride's second courthouse. The first went up in 1885—and burned down soon after. [Second time's the charm.] *305 W Colorado Ave*

THE DEPOT 1891
A true survivor. The railroad depot made the boom official. Since then, it's been repeatedly relocated, reconstructed, repurposed and rehabilitated. Yet its character remains. *300 S Townsend St*

NUGGET THEATRE BUILDING 1892
Designed by Denver architect James Murdoch. Style: Richardsonian Romanesque. Material: Red sandstone hewn from the hills above town. *201 W Colorado Ave*

TELLURIDE HISTORICAL MUSEUM 1895
Originally Dr. Hall's Hospital, built to treat miners and cowboys. The gurneys have been removed. The ghosts, allegedly, have not. *201 W Gregory Ave*

> "There may be other, older structures in town we don't know about yet. Every once and a while, a homeowner does a renovation, and when the walls are opened up, we find the house was once a log cabin." —Jonna Wensel, director, Historic Preservation Department

THE GOLD KING MINE AND AC ELECTRICITY

The first-long-distance transmission of alternating electric current [AC] took place in 1891 at the Ames Power Plant, about 6 miles from Telluride. The motive: to save the Gold King Mine, foundering due to high operating costs.

THE MINE
In 1887, Olaf Nelson, also known as the "Mighty Swede," staked the claim that would become the Gold King Mine. The Gold King was destined to ship more than 700,000 tons of gold and silver ore.

THE PLAN
Lucien L. Nunn, a carpenter, lawyer and the mine's majority stockholder, became convinced that electricity could revolutionize Gold King's operations. His brother, Paul, an electrical engineer, brought on Westinghouse Electric to create an alternating-current system. [Nunn would go on to found the Telluride Association and Deep Springs College, a self-governed two-year college in California.]

THE AC SYSTEM
Many young workers were brought in to build a dam and install steel piping to shoot water to a large Pelton water wheel. Using induction motor technology recently developed by Nikola Tesla, the AC system transmitted electricity 2.6 miles, from where two streams joined to form the San Miguel River, near the tiny town of Ophir.

THE PINHEADS
Nunn hired engineers from all over the country. Because he pinned each engineer's place of origin on a map, the engineers earned the nickname "pinheads."

In 2015, the Gold King Mine made a different kind of history: An epic spill—the result of a breached tailings dam—sent 3 million gallons of toxic wastewater spewing into the Animas River. The water contained high levels of lead, iron, arsenic and cadmium; the Animas ran an alarming deep yellow shade for several days. The mine is now a Superfund remediation site.

"ROCKY MOUNTAIN LOW"

In the summer of 1976, a drug bust rattled Telluride, where relations between conservative old-timers and the "hippie radicals" who had taken control of the town council had grown tense. Below, the opening of Roger Neville Williams' epic report on the case.

The little group was standing in front of the freshly painted Telluride Trappings and Toggery, admiring the brand-new striped awning. It's the kind of event that gets celebrated in Telluride: Terry Tice, store owner and city council member, popped open the champagne and the cork flew 60 feet in the air. Toasts were raised to the finest renovation on Colorado Avenue. As the group sipped and the glasses bubbled, the long, green Idarado Mining Company bus rumbled down the road, full of tired, vacant-eyed miners heading home. The driver motioned for the champagne drinkers to get out ol the way. As the mine bus went by, bartender Rick Silverman, who once debated Spiro Agnew on the David Frost Show shouted: "Just what these guys need. After working all day in the filthy mine, who do they get to see when they come through Telluride? A bunch of goddamn hippies standing in the middle of the street drinking champagne!" —*The Straight Creek Journal*, February 26, 1976

SELECTED CREATURES OF THE SAN JUAN MOUNTAINS

ELK
Some years, local herds linger along the Telluride Valley Floor, browsing vegetation.

CANADA LYNX
Recently reintroduced big cats prefer high-elevation forests of spruce and fir.

BOREAL OWL
Petite owl, brown with white spots. Listen for their whistle-y call: "Hoo-hoo-hoo-hoo-hoo!"

BIGHORN SHEEP
A herd roves between Telluride and Ridgway, ascending higher into the mountains come summer.

BEAVER
Furry, industrious dam-builders love to graze upon cottonwoods, willows and aspens.

BLACK BEAR
Lumbering, hibernating omnivores. Not always black—sometimes brown, even blonde.

BUTCH CASSIDY

Even famous bandits have to start somewhere. Cassidy made his outlaw debut in Telluride with a textbook heist of the San Miguel Bank.

1866	Robert Leroy Parker is born on a dusty Mormon homestead in southern Utah.
1870s	Parker takes work on a ranch and meets a cattle rustler named Mike Cassidy. Here, he learns the essentials: shooting straight and riding fast.
1884	Following whispers of silver, Parker rides to Telluride. Labors briefly at a mine before being accused of horse theft and splitting town.
1888	He returns to Telluride, this time racing horses for money, which he immediately blows in brothels and saloons.
1889	At age 23, Parker robs his first institution: Telluride's San Miguel Bank. He pays off the town marshall, then waltzes up to the desk with two accomplices, fellow Mormons. They hold the lone teller at gunpoint and demand $20,750. A waiting relay of fresh horses provides a clean getaway.
1890	He rebrands, taking Mike Cassidy's last name. Friends call him Butch, a nod to a stint carving beef in Wyoming.
1890s	Parker/Cassidy progresses to robbing banks and trains with the Wild Bunch gang and noted partner Harry Longbaugh, a.k.a. "The Sundance Kid." Steadily gains notoriety until his 1908 death in a shootout in Bolivia.

The 1969 film Butch Cassidy and the Sundance Kid *was [sadly] not shot in Telluride. Of the screenplay, writer William Goldman told the American Film Industry Archive: "The hardest part to make the story work was, Westerns are based on confrontation. Butch's whole life ... was about avoiding confrontation."*

THE NOTHING FESTIVAL

The story goes something like this: As Telluride's summer events proliferated, it came to pass that, by the early 1990s, but one festival-free summer weekend remained. And so was born a joke that, in turn, became its own festival for several years running. It included such events as "Sunrises and Sunsets as normal" and "Sense of humor search." Each year's festival T-shirt featured the festival motto on the back: "LEAVE ME ALONE." Below, highlights from the Nothing Festival's archived website, circa 2008.

STAFF

Since The Telluride Nothing Festival is really a "non festival," we have no need for a large expensive staff, or even a small cheap one. Usually festivals have Security staffs, but we have decided that instead of a "non security" staff, we will have an "Insecurity Staff." That way, everyone is qualified and will automatically become a staff member. No outsiders here!

PASSES

No permits or wristbands are needed here. If you want to look official, just tie a little piece of string around your wrist. Red color for backstage [if any], blue for camping, orange for all events, etc. If you want to look really silly, dress only in black and white, have a small placard on a string around your neck and don't forget the name tag.

PARKING

All parking regulations, including the dreaded solar powered parking meters, are in effect this weekend. We did ask the town to suspend metering this weekend for the fun of it and to show you folks visiting what is used to be like in a small town. Their response: "naaaaaaaaaaaah! We need the money." We locals think the meters are not really about parking. It's the revenue stream silly!

THE END! Despite the dryness and all the local things we like to make fun of, Telluride is still a great place to visit and live. Knock your socks off scenery and great weather. We celebrate the festival every year in July. Thank you for not participating!

ALMANAC

THE GRATEFUL DEAD

"Live Dead in Telluride"
By Michael Radosevich, Entertainer Editor
The Daily Sentinel, Grand Junction, August 21, 1987

Does one Grateful Dead concert make you a Dead Head? I think not, especially since I still don't own a tie-dyed T-shirt. But after attending my first ever Grateful Dead concert last Sunday, I'd sure go out of my way to see them again. Promoter Bill Graham is the reason the Grateful Dead played two dates last weekend in Telluride. He is also the reason both shows came off without a hitch.… During my short interview with Graham between the first and second set on Sunday, I saw him yell at a hired hand because there wasn't a trash can liner in one of the trash cans. There were empty trash bags stuck in the fence every three feet and by the time the concerts were over the town park was cleaner than it was before the Dead Heads even got there. I asked Graham what he thought about the setting for the concert. He just smiled and waved his hand around the valley and said, "not a bad canvas, is it?" Will the Grateful Dead ever play Telluride again? Graham said no, but if the people of Telluride ask him nicely, I think he might reconsider.

TELLURIDE AVALANCHE DOGS

Since 1986, dogs trained to sniff out avalanche victims buried beneath the snow have been key partners for the Telluride Ski Patrol. Some current and recent ski patrol canines:

PIKA Named for the small mousy mountain critters she shares her tan coloring with, and for late patroller Peter Inglis, known to friends as "Pi."

MONA Black Labrador retriever named for longtime patroller Mona Wilcox loves an alpine lake swim.

GRETCHEN This yellow Lab is a quick learner and a fan of curling up for naps by the woodstove at patrol headquarters.

LADY BEE As a puppy, her training was featured in a short kids' film. She hasn't let it go to her head.

THE GALLOPING GOOSE

In the late 19th century, the Rio Grande Southern Railroad built 162 miles of narrow-gauge track to connect mining towns Ouray, Durango and Telluride. After the silver market crashed amid the Great Depression, forcing the railroad to tighten its belt, the Galloping Goose, a "railbus" with a gasoline engine, was born. The Geese moved people, products and mail until operations ceased in 1951.

"The 'Galloping Goose' Saved Again"
The Daily Sentinel, March 23, 1945

Once again the "Galloping Goose" has had the death sentence commuted to "life for at least another year," and there is fresh hope that this famous shortline, narrow-gauge may yet achieve permanency; for prospects are good that mining and agricultural production in the region it serves, spurred by the war, will continue to develop in peace-time. The official name of this historic railway is the Rio Grande Southern, and, tho it has been in precarious health for years, the natural resources of the San Juan region, complemented by the resourcefulness of its progressive citizens, has prevented the road's abandonment. The loan from the Defense Supplies Corporation, that is presently saving the "Galloping Goose," is testimony to the value of the mineral and agricultural contributions it has been and is making to the war effort.

This 50-year-old short line has the distinction of having been saved by a woman. Prior to our entry into the war, but when our preparedness program had begun, the Rio Grande Southern was threatened with extinction; but Mrs. Elizabeth Pellet, state representative from Dolores county and one of the region's most prominent and progressive citizens, went to Washington and, thru a month's persistent wrangling, secured a $65,000 loan to keep the line operating. The new loan is confirmation of the arguments presented by Mrs. Pellet as to the value the road would be to our defense industries. The "Galloping Goose" runs thru some of the finest scenery not only in Colorado but in the nation, and, should it achieve a permanent and standardized existence, undoubtedly would become a popular route with sightseers when touring is again a popular pastime.

Today, Galloping Goose No. 4 is on display at the San Miguel County Courthouse in Telluride in summer, and is moved to the Ridgway Railroad Museum in winter.

THE SLATE

Leading up to Telluride's spring 1974 election, a group of young newcomers campaigned to take over the town council. This marked a sea change in a town already transformed by its then-new ski area.

"Slate Nabs 5 out of 7"
Telluride Times
April 4, 1974

On May 11, 1972, Joseph T. Zoline blew the whistle that started construction on the Telluride Ski Area. In the packed auditorium of the Nugget Theatre that afternoon there were mostly natives plus a few young people so new to town that they were almost like tourists. They had no political muscle and little social influence.

Last Tuesday, less than two years later, the young newcomers took over control of the town board with five out of the seven members including the mayor. Most of them had not even arrived in town that day two years before.

The Slate, the young newcomer group organized to put as big a brand as possible on the town hall, took the five posts, allowing only Bill Mahoney and Gary Bennett from the old board to keep their seats.

John Rosenfeld was expected to defeat Kathryn Evans but the margin of 360 to 191 surprised most everyone. In order after that were these members: Bill Mahoney, 358 [he was the high vote-getter on the board two years ago]; Fred Libby, 353; George Greenback and Gary Bennett tied with 300; John Roth, 258; and Terry Rice, 262....

Outgoing Mayor Raymond Fancher says that there will be no delay in the transition. He has called a meeting for 7 p.m. tonight at Town Hall to swear in the new members. "There's no use letting things slack off," Fancher said. "They might as well get their feet wet."

Though this article doesn't use the word "hippie" to describe the newcomers, many people at the time did. On June 27, when The Telluride Times *ran a full spread of headshots introducing the new council, the headline read: "IS THIS THE ESTABLISHMENT? Or the cast from 'Hair'?"*

THE GREAT FLOOD OF 1914

When dark clouds first rolled over Telluride on July 27, 1914, no one realized that the most destructive weather event in local history lurked just around the corner. At noon, the sky opened, dropping curtains of rain over the Liberty Bell Mine Complex north of town. Less than an hour later, mine workers cried out: A 50-foot surge of water was pouring down the mountainside. It swamped the mine's waste dump, taking with it thousands of tons of crushed rock and debris. The mudslide gathered speed as it tumbled into nearby Cornet Creek, splintering a dam and hurtling toward town. Residents heard the roar of the flood before they saw it. Some homes were crushed outright. Others were lifted from their foundations and carried along with the swell. The next day, *The Salida Mail* reported 112 buildings destroyed, two residents killed and 700 left homeless. Colorado Avenue was buried in debris 10 feet deep. Mud filled the Sheridan Hotel nearly up to the ceiling. It took months to clear the sludge. A century later, memories of the flood—and a sense of pride in the town's resilience—continue to be passed down.

UTE HISTORY

Over 1,000 years before tourists built second homes, the Uncompaghre Utes summered in Telluride. They hunted deer and grouse, reaped the benefits of the bountiful river and appreciated the wandering wildlife on the valley floor. Ute lore details a dream in which a tribesman woke a sleeping bear well past its spring alarm. He feared starvation for the bear. With thanks, the large mammal led the man into the forest, where bears danced to the tune of winter's end. The annual spring Bear Dance is a Ute celebration of the awakening of bears and a mutual friendship. [A drum beats slowly, three steps forward and three steps back.] Despite contemporary Ute influence and presence across the San Juan Mountains, San Miguel County did not initiate attempts at reconciliation with the area's Indigenous community until 2014. The people of the Shining Mountains are still here; discover more at the Ute Indian Museum in Montrose, Colorado.

SKIING ORIGINS

"Telluride Should Have Ski Club, Says Champion Ski Jumper,"
The Daily Journal, April 10, 1923

That Telluride should have a ski club and that conditions here are ideal for several months of the finest winter sport imaginable, is the opinion of Lars Haugen, champion ski jumper of America. Mr. Haugen was a visitor in Telluride on Saturday and is enthusiastic about skiing conditions in this section. He is a booster for skiing and believes that Telluride should have a real live active ski club that might in the course of a year or two promote a ski tournament which would attract as much attention as the now famous Steamboat Springs tournament which is held each year. Mr. Haugen, who is traveling in the interests of the Northland Ski company, was a business visitor in Telluride Saturday. While stopping here for the day he secured a pair of skis and went over to Bear Creek, where he reported the snow was still fair for skiing, and where he says there are several places ideally suited for a ski course. Mr. Haugen of course believes there is no other sport which compares with skiing, and says that Telluride people with their long winter and ideal natural ski courses should form a club and get into the outdoors during the winter. So enthusiastic was Mr. Haugen that a number of local people who like skiing are already considering plans for starting a club next fall. In the event any interest is shown in Telluride early next winter, Mr. Haugen can be induced to come here and assist with getting the club started and possibly give an exhibition. He is the world's champion ski jumper and has broken many records and won many prizes and honors. … While there is no opportunity at this time to start a ski club, yet this matter should be kept in mind and early next winter some plan should be started to sound out local people on the advisability of starting such a club. There seems no doubt but the plan would work out to splendid advantage here, and would furnish much splendid healthful outdoor exercise and sport for Telluride people during the winter months.

Lars Haugen, born in Norway's Telemark region, became an eminent figure in the formative days of American alpine culture. Along with his brother Anders [a U.S. Olympian], Haugen also helped establish skiing at Lake Tahoe and elsewhere.

ALPINE LAKES OF NOTE

BLUE LAKE
Set deep in Bridal Veil Basin, overlooking Telluride. The trail to the lake meanders through mining ruins, wildflower clusters and past Bridal Veil Falls, the tallest free-falling waterfall in the state. *Colorado Avenue, east of Pandora Mine*

TROUT LAKE
At 9,716 feet, surrounded by Sheep Mountain, Vermilion Peak, Golden Horn and Pilot Knob. Paddleboarding and picnicking in summer, cross-country skiing in winter. *Highway 145 to County Road 63A*

HOPE LAKE
Tucked away above Trout Lake, at 10,789 feet. Between the two, wildflowers guide the trail through creek crossings and views of the surrounding Lizard Head Wilderness. *Highway 145 to Forest Road 627*

ALTA LAKES
Worth the dirt-road trek to see the emerald-green waters reflect the mountains all around [and check out the ghost town along the way]. Sleep above 11,000 feet at Alta Lakes Observatory. *Highway 145 to Alta Lakes Road*

BLUE LAKES
Beneath Mount Sneffels, three high-alpine lakes color the mountains turquoise against a backdrop of ashy scree. Not to be confused with Bridal Veil's Blue Lake. *Colorado Highway 62 to Dallas Creek Road*

ISLAND LAKE
At 12,400 feet in elevation, Island Lake is far from the Caribbean, but the green and blue hues lend a tropical feel. From here, it's a steep 4-mile hike to Upper Ice Lake Basin. *Highway 550 to Forest Service Road 585*

COLUMBINE LAKE
The hike is 8 miles round-trip, and steep. But the reward: The expansive basin and piercing blue of Columbine Lake. Why so blue? Fine sediment runoff from glaciers eroding. *Highway 550 to Forest Service Road 679*

INCLUDED

044-046 SUMMER ADVENTURES
Sure, it's a ski town. But summer brings these mountains to life in a different way, offering endless adventure.

047-049 THE BLUEBIRD SKI DAY
Bright mornings, sun-washed afternoons and the all-important après: a perfect session on the slopes.

050-052 THE ARTS
A town suffused with creativity finds just the right mix of rugged edge and aesthetic sophistication.

053-055 OUT-THERE LODGING
Beyond Telluride's cozy streets, intriguing outposts give shelter to modern-day explorers.

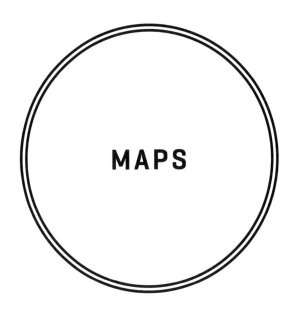

MAPS

Pictorial journeys through unique Telluride culture, commerce and landscape by illustrator Abigail Fox. Not to scale.

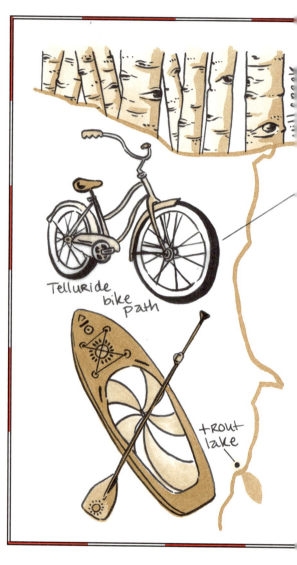

SUMMER ADVENTURES

Telluride's slender gravy boat of a valley cradles a lifetime's worth of exploration.

TELLURIDE VIA FERRATA

Telluride's "iron way" clings to the sheer west face of Ajax Peak. The intrepid can pick their way across the iron rungs, bolts and cables for an airy 2-mile traverse. [Guide recommended. Try Mountain Trip.] Also known as the "Krogerata" in honor of Chuck Kroger, local climber and dreamer behind its construction. *Bridal Veil Falls Rd*

CORNET CREEK FALLS

Cornet spans 80 feet of open air, a free-hanging ribbon of water cupped in a red-rock amphitheater. Better yet: it's just a quarter mile from town. *North Aspen Street*

BALLARD MOUNTAIN

The wildflower-specked summit affords spin-around views of the San Juans. Of course, such a prize must be earned: 4,000 feet of elevation gain should just about do it. *Forest Service Rd 648*

MILL CREEK BIKE TRAILS

Crisp singletrack hides in plain sight. Trace wooded contours on the Mill Creek Waterline trail. Level 2: Target the Deep Creek Trail for a 7.5-mile masterclass in high-altitude riding. *Mill Creek Road*

TELLURIDE BIKE PATH

This greenway threads the Valley Floor, offering nearly 7 miles of paved cruising in the shadow of the San Juans. To make it a loop, catch the San Miguel River Trail and circle back to your car. *700 W Pacific Ave*

TROUT LAKE

Come fall, reflected aspens gild the lake's surface, giving the illusion of paddling through gold. SUPs, kayaks and swimmers welcome. Camp at nearby Priest Lake to streamline the journey between sleeping bag and boat. Trails transform into Nordic nirvana in winter. *North Trout Lake Road*

BY THE BOOK *Susan Kees first published the* Telluride Hiking Guide *in 1992, after almost three decades of strolling the San Juans. Now in its third edition, the book remains a beloved companion.*

THE BLUEBIRD SKI DAY

From a fresh corduroy lap with sweeping views to a deserved glass of wine at nearly 12,000 feet.

COFFEE COWBOY
Before you put your skis on, find the evergreen horse trailer to get your morning caffeine uplift. A frothy Annie Oakley and a Mesa Rose Kitchen burrito: ideal fuel for your day on the hill.
300 W San Juan Ave

CHAIR 9
Plunge Lift, as it's known, is the ideal place to "plunge" into the first runs of a truly epic day. This long chairlift got a makeover in 2022, cutting travel time in half, to just 6.5 minutes.

BLACK IRON BOWL
Like many places around here, Black Iron Bowl takes its name from an old mining claim. Expert terrain abounds, from a quick jaunt down Genevieve slope to a lengthy hike up Palmyra Peak. Between, the boot-pack courses along a ridge where chutes, couloirs and open glades ski like a sigh of relief.

SEE FOREVER
Cascading down from the top of the resort, skiers whip by trees on Lift 14's famous run. On clear days, views extend all the way to Utah's La Sal Range, some 80 miles away.

ALPINO VINO
Nestled alongside See Forever, a European-style hut awaits, with leisurely daybeds, sheepskin throws, a wood-burning fireplace and views of faraway peaks. Can a glass of red and a charcuterie board be lunch? In this fairy-tale spot, we'll go with yes.
12100 Camels' Garden Rd

OAK
No such day is complete without après, local-style, next to Lift 8: Skis dumped, dogs parked on the patio, flung-off layers and tables pushed together to share adventure stories and plates of barbecue. Oh, and margaritas too.
250 W San Juan Ave

BACKCOUNTRY TIPS *Before you head out, tune in to* The San Juan Snowcast *for up-to-date information on "what's going on in the sky and on the ground," every winter.*

The Arts

Nugget theater

ah haa school for the arts

slate gray gallery

MiXX projects + atelier

THE ARTS

This small but wildly creative community nurtures a wide range of cultural institutions old and new.

SHERIDAN OPERA HOUSE
Small historic music venue has hosted major names like Taj Mahal and Jackson Browne. Built in 1913, with floral stenciling that hovers between Craftsman style and art nouveau. *110 N Oak St*

SLATE GRAY GALLERY
Contemporary art exhibitions showcase the work of local, regional and international artists. *130 E Colorado Ave*

THE NUGGET THEATRE
L.L. Nunn built the red sandstone Nugget Building in 1892. Today, home to the Telluride Film Festival, including special indie screenings year-round. Great popcorn. *207 W Colorado Ave*

TELLURIDE TRANSFER WAREHOUSE
In 2017, Telluride Arts purchased the onetime transportation hub. It's now set to become a community cultural center, designed to maintain the existing architecture while adding a roof deck and movable elements to accommodate a range of events. *201 S Fir St*

MOUNTAINFILM
Telluride is a fitting base for this festival, featuring documentary films about outdoor adventure, adrenaline seeking and environmental activism from around the world. Held every Memorial Day weekend. *122 S Oak St*

MIXX PROJECTS + ATELIER
Airy gallery and shop where art meets design. Gorgeous handcrafted jewelry, stylish furniture, paintings. *307 E Colorado Ave*

AH HAA SCHOOL FOR THE ARTS
Founded by writer and bookmaker Daniel Tucker in 1990, creativity hub hosts classes in printmaking, ceramics, textiles and more. Home of the American Academy of Bookbinding too. *155 W Pacific Ave*

LOCAL ORG *In addition to supporting the arts in town, the nonprofit Telluride Arts produces events such as the Arts Bazaar and Art Walk. Its website also features an extensive artist directory.* telluridearts.org

OUT-THERE LODGING

Beyond Telluride, unconventional places to lay your head beckon: rustic ski huts to restorative hot-springs resorts.

THE OBSERVATORY AT ALTA LAKES
Locals built this remote three-story chalet with stone and logs in the 1970s. Five decades later, it remains a dreamy place, hidden away at the edge of Telluride Ski Resort, with national forest all around. *4665 Alta Lakes Rd, Ophir*

BRIDAL VEIL BACKCOUNTRY SKI CAMP
At 12,500 feet, this is the ideal base camp for world-class backcountry skiing. Heated tents for ski touring in style. Come evening, enjoy catered meals, epic stargazing and rollicking bonfires. *helitrax.com*

CAMP V
1940s uranium mining outpost transformed into a boutique camp spot with unique on-site art installations. Airstreams, jupes, furnished safari and Lotus Belle tents, mining company homes reimagined as chic cabins. *Ee 26 Rd, Vancorum*

BASECAMP 550
Small campground with RV sites, glamping tents and casitas amid the San Juan Mountains' grandeur. Carouse with fellow travelers in the cozy clubhouse. *20725 U.S. 550, Ridgway*

DUNTON HOT SPRINGS
"Restored 1800s ghost town" might not sound like a luxury resort description, but trust us. Nestled in an alpine valley along the West Dolores River, Dunton, with its cabins, saloon, trails and of course hot springs [both indoor and outdoor, ranging in temperature from 85°F to 106°F], is the dreamiest soaking spot around. *8532 Road 38, Dolores*

LAST DOLLAR SKI HUT
One of a system of huts from Telluride to Ouray, traversing the Sneffels Range, each with a propane cookstove, woodstove and bunk beds for eight. *sanjuanhuts.com*

BIKE TRIP: *The San Juan Hut System includes accommodations for hiking and mountain biking too. The Telluride to Moab bike trip is easy enough for first-time riders. sanjuanhuts.com/mtb/telluride-moab*

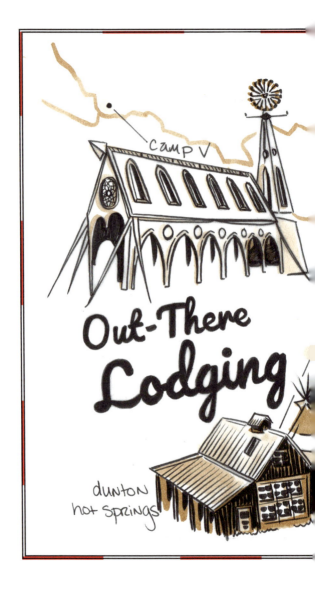

INCLUDING

058 *Art Goodtimes*
060 *Kathy Green*
063 *Lisa Issenberg*
064 *Rick Trujillo*
065 *Matt Steen*
066 *Harry Kearney*
068 *Maria "Lupita" Esquivel*
069 *Jane Watenpaugh*
071 *Geneva Shaunette*

INTERVIEWS

―

Nine conversations with locals of note about avalanche science, poetry, trail running, metalworking, snowboarding, restaurant life and the beauty of small-town politics

INTERVIEWS

ART GOODTIMES

POET, POLITICIAN

I REALLY BELIEVE the arts are what make us most human.

FIRST YEAR I was here, I had a poetry reading. I think two people showed up.

I GOT a job as arts council director. It paid $5 an hour. But I was living in a wreck down in Placerville that cost like $50 a month.

I'VE BEEN TO millions of readings, open mics. Nobody listens to anybody. Well, not much.

WITH TALKING GOURDS, we do a sharing circle. We actually listen to each other. Tou have the gourd, you have the floor.

IF PEOPLE WANT to do a poem, great. Or maybe they want to sing a song.

WE NOW HAVE a strong audience for poetry in this tiny, dinky town, which is pretty amazing.

I'VE BEEN THE poet in residence for the Telluride Mushroom Festival for 43 years, which is the longest I've done anything in my life.

IN TELLURIDE, if you have interest and ambition, you can make something happen, whether it's music, or painting, or any of the arts, even though it's very expensive here to live.

I WAS A county commissioner for 20 years, first elected in '96.

I WOULD'VE LOVED to have been able to make a rule that you had to live in the home for six to eight months a year.

THAT WOULD HAVE changed things. I couldn't get the backing.

I WAS A GREEN in a town that's way Democrat. People liked who I was. They didn't care about the party.

MY NAME IN Italian is Arturo Bontempi. But I use the English. It means "good times."

IS IT MY real name? Yeah, it's translated, but it's real.

INTERVIEWS

KATHY GREEN

BUILDER, ARTIST

PEOPLE ALWAYS tell me they wish they were here in the early '80s. And I just start laughing.

IF YOU WANT to go back to what it was like, just turn off your telephone, your computers, your TV, your gas heat. It was like camping out, kind of.

BUT IT WAS fun. There was a great sense of community.

WE WENT TO all three movies each week, because the movies were heated.

WE HAD PARTIES to go get firewood in the summer. Five or 10 of us would go out with pickup trucks.

WE'D FIX a big potluck dinner inside and split and stack all the wood outside. Then the next day, we'd go to a different house.

IN TELLURIDE, for many people of my generation, the way in was to buy an extreme fixer-upper.

EVERYBODY BOUGHT the cheapest, junky, falling-down wrecks of houses and remodeled them.

CHUCK AND I first drove into Telluride on a September afternoon.

BRIGHT yellow leaves, bright blue sky, not a cloud in sight— and the sound of hammers.

WE MOVED HERE in April of '79. Built our first spec house in 1980.

WE CALLED OUR company BONE Construction—Back of Nowhere Engineering—based on that Edward Abbey name that's similar.

WE LEARNED A lot about mountain-town rentals. The good, the bad and the ugly.

AT FIRST WE were doing little remodels. Then we started building bigger houses, brand-new houses.

AND WE STARTED doing a lot of historic remodels, which I really loved.

GOING INTO the house, you had to rip everything out to get down to the bones, to see if the structure was going to be strong enough.

IT WAS INTERESTING to watch the houses grow in size and complexity.

I'VE BEEN ON the Planning and Zoning Board for 40 years. Doing that in tandem with building helped me understand what was going to work.

WHEN DANIEL TUCKER came to town in the summer of '91, he started the Ah Haa School for the Arts.

THAT'S HOW I discovered fabric dyeing, which really resonated with me. I was like, *OK, this is paint mixing, but it goes on fabric and it's more fun.*

I LIKE THINGS that are spontaneous. Things where perfection might not be the goal.

AND I LIKE surprises: when you've dyed this thing and it might be all bundled up in many kinds of shibori folds or clamps or ties or whatever. You undo it, and then you see what you've gotten.

IF YOU TRIED to do it on purpose, you couldn't do it. I love that aspect of fabric dyeing.

SOON I STARTED teaching at Ah Haa.

IT REALLY FILLED some gaps in my life. And it let me be a little bolder, sometimes, on the houses.

I COULD SAY, "I am an art instructor, and I think this …" Very gently guide them away from something I was not seeing.

MY HUSBAND CHUCK died in 2007 of pancreatic cancer.

HE WAS A CLIMBER, and one of the last things he did before he got sick was build the via ferrata here. That has become his legacy.

I HELPED MAKE the original rungs, in the basement of our house.

I HAVE A FEAR of heights, so I've never done the entire via ferrata, which is fine.

DOWN THE MIDDLE is when it gets very vertical and you're crossing a sheer cliff.

THAT'S THE PART I happily don't go near.

INTERVIEWS

LISA ISSENBERG

METALWORKER

EVERYTHING I DO is custom. It's not a great business model. People have suggested, "Can't you just come up with your stock item?" But that's not in my heart.

I PUT A LOT of energy into *How far can I take this?*

I STARTED KIITELLÄ in 2012, when I decided to go hardcore into just awards. It's Finnish for "to thank, praise and applaud."

MOUNTAINFILM was the first to hire me for awards.

I'D COME UP with designs, and it was always a win-win: they were honoring people, and I was a part of that.

FOR THE FIRST Mountainfilm Awards I did, the theme was Tibet. I made vertical prayer flags with mild steel.

FOR THE 2022 Winter X Games, the theme was aspen trees. I used slices of aspens that had already been downed by weather—wind, avalanche.

IT'S NICE TO take direction from the material.

MY IDEAS COME from past inspirations, past design periods, art, color and nature.

I'M TOTALLY influenced by Bauhaus. Everything's super clean.

WHAT I'M BILLING does not always cover where my heart and head go.

HAPPINESS IS connecting with people, and that's more important sometimes.

THIS HAS TURNED out to be the perfect path for me: Taking the clean perfection of industrial processes and bringing it into my shop, and adding the handcraft and the soul. The ripped skin and the sweat and the energy.

EVEN THOUGH I'm in my middle years, I always feel like I'm just starting.

I JUST NOW feel like I'm getting somewhere.

INTERVIEWS

RICK TRUJILLO

MOUNTAIN RUNNER

THE SAN JUAN Mountains—well, they're just home.

THE IMOGENE PASS Run began because of a missed connection and a chance encounter.

ALL MY RUNS are mountains, period. I can't run on flat ground. That was my methodology of training for mountain races.

I DECIDED, why not try Imogene Pass?

TUESDAY, August 6, 1974, here's my diary: *Telluride run via Imogene.* I left at 5:12 p.m., after work. I was working at a mine in Ouray.

A FRIEND OF mine was supposed to meet me in Telluride.

I ARRIVE AND my friend is nowhere to be seen. I'm walking up and down Main Street, and all I have is my T-shirt, shorts and running shoes.

I BUMPED INTO two skiers I knew. They were amazed to learn I had run from Ouray.

ONE WAS Jerry Race, a pharmacist. He was a member of the Chamber of Commerce.

THE CHAMBER STARTED the race as a gimmick to try to get people to come to Telluride.

THE FIRST RACE, there were seven starters and six finishers.

NOW WE HAVE 1,100 to 1,300 starters every year.

IN '85, eight inches of snow fell over the course of the race.

I WALKED ALL the way up to the top of the pass to blaze a trail for the runners, and to be there yelling "This is the pass!"

BECAUSE ABOVE about 12,000 feet, it was whiteouts.

THE LAST TIME I ran it was in 2018. I was 70.

IT USED TO be a lark for me.

BUT BOY, I tell you: I had to work to get over to Telluride.

MATT STEEN

AVALANCHE FORECASTER, SKI GUIDE

EVERYONE KNOWS THAT I'm a snow geek.

YOU GO OUT, walk down the street and someone's going to start talking to you about the wind or whatever they saw.

I ALWAYS LOOKED up to the ski patrol and the avalanche forecasters. I aspired to be that tuned in to the snowpack.

YOU GATHER ALL this information, and you try to figure out: What are the chances you're going to trigger an avalanche?

JUST HAVING YOUR radar up, tuning in to the right things and tuning out other things—I guess that's a little bit of wizardry.

YOU ERR ON the side of caution. I know of retired forecasters who still have nightmares.

THE LAST 10 years, I've worked with Telluride Helitrax. Sleep in your own bed, drive five minutes to the office, which has a helipad behind it—it's insane.

WE ARE A rare operator that has an explosives permit and the capabilities of slope testing with explosives.

I'VE THROWN a lot of explosives in my career.

THE SAN JUANS are an interesting place to study snow. They are particularly avalanche-y. In the Southwest, we're geographically closer to a warmer climate, but our elevation is just as high as the other highest mountainous regions in the lower Rocky Mountains.

WHAT WE GET is a continental snowpack, which means it's shallow and generalized as weak.

WE HAVE BIG, fluctuating temperature swings from night and day and throughout the season, which transforms the snow crystals in the snowpack and can weaken them.

LEARNING THE MOUNTAINS like it's your backyard is a very special thing.

HARRY KEARNEY

PRO SNOWBOARDER

I WAS SIX years old when my family moved to Telluride.

GROWING UP, it was mellow. There was the safety net of the community.

EVERYBODY'S parents know each other, and everybody knows everyone's parents. So you could just run around and do whatever.

BUT IF YOU were causing trouble, your parents would hear about it before you got home.

I WENT TO Mountain School. It was started by a bunch of parents who just wanted to take their kids camping, and it was mostly outside.

WITH SNOWBOARDING, Hagen being the older brother, it all kind of came from him.

WE BOTH GREW up competing out here.

HE'S ABOUT A YEAR and a quarter older—just far enough that the way the age divisions are set up, we were separate. Which I think is a good thing.

THE FIRST TIME I won the Mt. Baker Banked Slalom, that was rad. I was 17.

I WAS AWAY for eight years or so, up in Washington. Bellingham was great, but it was kind of too big for me.

I CAME BACK to Telluride because of family. And just the familiarity and the ease of it.

AND HONESTLY, to walk to the lifts is insane.

I'M ALSO A fly-fishing guide.

IN THE MAIN season, I could work every day. Even on your days off, you're getting calls because it's so busy.

YOU'RE DIRECTLY involved with the mountains just by living here.

IT'S GNARLY sometimes. It can be totally tragic.

AND IT CAN be so awesome. It's just so ingrained in your day-to-day life.

I JUST LOVE that; I haven't been anywhere else where your surroundings are like that.

INTERVIEWS

MARIA "LUPITA" ESQUIVEL

RESTAURANT MANAGER

WHEN MY FAMILY made the trip from Zacatecas, Mexico, in 2001, I was 10 years old. I didn't know any English.

.....

ALL I KNEW was that we were going to some town in Colorado, where it was going to be snowy.

.....

I LIKED GROWING up here. Getting older, in high school, there were times when I didn't like it. I was like, *What is this place?*

.....

AFTER HIGH SCHOOL, I really enjoyed snowboarding. So I stayed, and I learned to appreciate the place more.

.....

I'VE WORKED AT La Cocina de Luz for nine years.

.....

IT'S MELLOW. You can crack a joke with somebody over the counter.

.....

I LIKE THE enchiladas: shredded beef with the green sauce.

.....

THE BEANS ARE really good. Anasazi beans. They're local, out of Dove Creek.

.....

TORTILLAS, corn or flour, they're both local. Good-quality ingredients, all organic.

.....

WORKING IN THE restaurant, I don't see many of the Hispanic workers that provide so much for the industry.

.....

BEING A Mexican restaurant, I feel like we should be seeing a lot more familiar faces.

.....

I GUESS BECAUSE I grew up here, I didn't really realize until I was older that Telluride is full of white people. That's just what America was.

.....

HOUSING HAS GOTTEN super tough, super expensive.

.....

EVERYBODY'S moving out, and people don't want to commute.

.....

IT CAN'T BE good for anybody to just work, work, work, commute.

.....

A LOT OF the time, I wish I had more friends that I could use my Spanglish with, and joke around and they would get my joke.

JANE WATENPAUGH

FORMER SKI PATROLLER

I WAS THE first woman ski patroller.

I DO LOOK back and go, *Wow, that was important*. It was right at the time of Gloria Steinem and Women's Lib.

I WORKED AT the medical clinic, and I'd gotten my E.M.T. I went to Johnnie Stevens, who was head of ski patrol, and I said, "Johnny, I'd like to be on the slopes."

THIS WAS '76, '77. That year it didn't snow. I only worked eight days.

THE FIRST FIVE years, we didn't have snowmaking, so we would haul snow. We'd shovel it into toboggans off the side of the trails and dump it.

IT WOULDN'T EVEN last the whole day.

SKI PATROL WAS a boys' club for sure. You skied all day and drank all night. The Sheridan was our bar.

I ALWAYS SAY ski patrol was my favorite job, but mother was pretty great. And grandmother maybe trumps them all.

BOY, I'M STILL in love with this place. I skied 83 days last year.

I HAVE A great, tight group of women my age that I ski winter with and hunt with in summer.

JANE'S RULES, this is number one: You have to ski six runs to count the day.

AND THEN THERE are so many rules about what can really be considered a run.

IT'S FUNNY, my girlfriends feel really guilty if they don't ski six runs and then count the day.

WHEN I SOCIALIZE with my girlfriends, it's never over coffee. It's always on the trail or on the ski lift. And that's my psychiatrist, my therapy session.

THERE'S SOME MAGIC here. That's all I can say.

INTERVIEWS

GENEVA SHAUNETTE

TOWN COUNCIL MEMBER, BAR MANAGER

I MOVED TO Telluride when I was 22. This was during the recession. It was not hard to find a place to live.

EVERYBODY LIVED IN old five-bedroom ski-bum houses that hadn't been knocked down and remodeled yet, with wood burning stoves. And it was cozy.

YOU COULD PAY $300 and live in a walk-in closet somewhere.

I ALWAYS TOLD myself I would stay for two winters and two summers and then probably go learn to sail or go do this somewhere else.

BUT MY LIFE kept getting better, so I didn't leave.

MY WIFE AND I started our little event company, Back Pocket Creative, doing wedding pop-ups and stuff, and we started The Down-Low, the storytellers night.

THE TOUGH JOB that we have as council people is trying to balance what's best for the whole community.

THERE'S NO ANSWER that's going to save everyone.

THE BIGGEST ISSUE that we're really all arguing about at the end of the day is: Who is Telluride for?

AND HOW TO make it the best for those people.

I REALLY RESPECT and love the democratic process.

I'LL GET INTO this really intense thing at council with a group of people, and then over the weekend, there's an opera show at the Telluride Transfer Warehouse.

I'M MAKING DRINKS for these people who hate what I'm doing, but they still are polite and enjoy chatting with me.

THAT'S THE BEST: when we can put that aside and enjoy a cocktail at a show in the beautiful town that we love.

I'VE GOT AN old Vanagon. It's the one that's painted like a zebra.

INCLUDED

074 **FREE RIDE**
By Daiva Chesonis

080 **SINGING INTO THIN AIR**
By Emily Scott Robinson

084 **THREE POEMS**
By Rosemerry Wahtola Trommer

088 **FROM "HIGH-ALTITUDE ATHLETICS"**
By David Lavender

STORIES

Essays and selected writing from noted Telluride voices

STORIES

FREE RIDE

Written by **DAIVA CHESONIS**

BUILDING CHAIRLIFTS was not in the plan.

Armed with a degree in Russian studies, I meant to go to grad school and then free the republics from the Soviet Union. Neither looked like an easy job. Hailing from Baltimore, all it took was one summer of living in the less-humid Laurel Highlands of southwestern Pennsylvania to fall in love with the mountain lifestyle, convincing me to stay a bit longer before hitting the books again. I bought a mountain bike, started climbing and running rivers and creeks, and in 1990, I went to work for the Cable Transportation Engineering Corporation [CTEC], building lifts at cute little ski areas in the mid-Atlantic states.

The job meant waiting for a call every March, to learn what resort you'd get to know from the inside out as you enhanced its reach, capacity and experience. In early 1992, I found out I'd be moving from the small stuff to a two-year gig in Telluride, to build a gondola transportation system that would connect the old mining town and the much newer Mountain Village. I recall that the job boss was very clear about this being a historic build: the first in the nation constructed to improve air quality, it would transport skiers and commuters alike—and it would be free to ride.

I rolled in [er, climbed up] to Telluride on June 3, in a packed-to-the-gills Isuzu Trooper. Work on the G would begin a couple of days later, starting at an altitude of 10,540 feet. Hello, harsh headache for this lowlander, simply trying to breathe at that crisp altitude without proper acclimatization.

The process for building lifts is something like that for a house: foundation, walls, beams, roof, weathervane—but instead, footers, towers, sheave wheels, cable, chairs. In the case of a detachable gondola, the "chairs" are expensive computer-wired cabins. Deep rectangular holes were dug for the concrete vaults at each of the three stations, plus smaller square versions under each tower. So much rebar hauled to each spot. Diggers and cranes with outriggers sitting at precarious angles: an ordinary scene. Once the footers were all in and cured, it was time to erect the ever-growing rows of green-painted steel arriving daily by semi to our boneyard—then a dirt lot, now the Franz Klammer Lodge. There's only one way to do that: call in a helicopter.

Tower day, a day most lift builders live for. Progress on steroids.

Flown by uber-precise position pilots, many of them ex-military, these choppers are fitted with a bug-eyed bubble window for their head to be able to see the task—and us—from above. For each of our crew of six, the task meant hands-on wrestling hole-punched tower bases onto long upright mega-bolts sticking out of the concrete, all while the tower is connected by steel cable to a hovering chopper. Then, putting a washer in place, spinning a thick nut from our belt pouch down the bolt in a choreographed effort to stabilize it enough before the pilot gets an OK from the ground to mechanically detach.

Imagine the cacophonous rotor wash, dust and leaflitter swirling around, as you try to accomplish this team feat within about three minutes. Once the cable releases, the heli swoops down to base for another tower, while we hop-skip-jump from one steep, grassy hummock down to another to be in position to receive again. Ears tune in to the *wump-wump-wump*, indicating how little time we have before the next tower swings overhead and the rush of time and adrenaline replays itself. The only real break—a chance to reload pre-cached washers and nuts and maybe chug some water—came when the helicopter refueled at the Telluride airport. Writing this 30-plus years later, my stomach still flips with nervousness. It was truly one of the most exciting workdays I've ever had.

For sure, there were other exhilarating heli-days: to set crossarms, then the grooved sheave wheel trains, plus haul ropes and communication lines. The on-the-ground splice day deserves a poem of its own. And finally, load testing, and taking our first crew ride, myself part of a duo that logged the G's first onboard kiss. But for me, tower day takes the cake.

Fast-forward to March 2021. When the rest of the crew moved on to Park City in 1996 to build lifts for the 2002 Olympics, I'd given up my lift-building career and decided to stay in Telluride. In the interim, I've gone through several iterations, including co-owner of Between the Covers Bookstore and poet laureate of San Miguel County. The latter brought me full circle to the stage at the gondola's 25th anniversary gala—complete with a cake sporting a motorized gondola—to recite my original poem

STORIES

"The Splice of Life." Think of it and the amount of labor and thrill-filled devotion to exactness by its builders next time you sail through the air for 13 minutes as one of its annual three million riders. May it forever be free.

THE SPLICE OF LIFE

Once upon a time
in a cul-de-sac in the sky
an old-timer and a newcomer met.
They enjoyed each other's company;
one shared the old tales, the other, new dreams.

Growing old can be painful ...
wise creaky bones betelling of use, woodstoves and boardwalks part of their past.

Being new? Also kinda painful ...
buttslapped into life on a rolling-sloped ranch, growth charts and tee times a nod to its future.

Not everyone wanted the baby in the highchair.
Not everyone listened to the prospector on the bench. A fixed grip of stances could only hurt,
a detached attitude would keep folks in cars.

That curvy Lawson Hill has claimed lives.

Mind the gap, someone thought ...
Let's engineer a ropeway!
Let's make it clean ... and free!
Let's sink a loveline into the palm of this place.

String theory at its best.

They arrived in June of '92, stoked for the challenge that steep slopes and wetlands provide.
The crew from all over set up their boneyard
in the dusty skiers' parking lot and they got to work.

STORIES

There were 10-hour days and 6-day weeks.
There were gnarly injuries and some nights in the Montrose jail when
    O'Bannon's got them too crazy on their one night off.
None of them were local
but they felt the vibe, understood the mission:

Connect and play nice.

Digging footer holes and setting towers is one thing, that loveline is
    a whole 'nother.

Pretty sure that 99.9% of riders never think about the cable from
    which those cabins dangle.
How it came on big spools on really big trucks.
Steel threads wound about each other and then those, wound about
    again, the girth and weight a woven wow.

They don't think about how it didn't arrive as a closed loop, how it
    needed to be joined,
married like a miner and a ski bunny,
til death do they part.

That wedding was the trick of a magician of precision, brought in at
    top dollar, an officiant worth every dime. Making ends   meet,
    infinity and safety squared.

It's simply tension.
Two ends of oiled threads unbraided
only to be expertly rebraided,
a meshing meant for movement.
Once lifted into the smooth groove of the sheave wheels, two towns
    were now in bed.

It's called a splice and it means the world when defying gravity while
    floating cleanly thru trees en route to meetings or pow, a long
    shift ... or memorials.
It means the world to a world that's choking.

That couple, the old-timer and the newcomer? They're doing just fine
   in that forever-weighted pull. It makes them stronger every day.
Connected but separate.
Unified but unique.
It's what we dream of when we dream of love.

DAIVA CHESONIS has been a snowboard instructor, owner/operator of Vision Design, art director at *Telluride Magazine* and, most recently, co-owner of Between the Covers Bookstore. She founded the Telluride AIDS Benefit Fashion Show and the Telluride Literary Arts Festival. From 2109 to 2022 she served as San Miguel County poet laureate.

STORIES

SINGING INTO THIN AIR

Written by **EMILY SCOTT ROBINSON**

I WAS A fresh-faced 24-year-old at my first Telluride Bluegrass Festival, in the summer of 2012. The high-country sun was hot, and the San Juan Mountains cradled me and several thousand music fans in a natural amphitheater under bluebird skies. I spent four days barefoot in the grass, buzzed on New Belgium beer, listening to barn-burning fiddle solos and beautiful songwriting. John Prine was on the bill that summer, and I got to see my hero live for the first time ever. In the afternoons, I wandered home to nap, leaving my windows open so I could still hear the music floating through the air. In the evenings, I carried a sleeping bag out to the field and lay underneath the stars until the last notes rang off the canyon walls. As that lyric of John's says, "How lucky can one man get?"

It didn't take me long to understand why people drove from every state in the union to come to what locals just call "Bluegrass." It's the pinnacle festival of summer and a beloved tradition, going strong since 1973. I was new to Telluride—a North Carolina native who'd taken a full-time job as a social worker, moving sight unseen to this gorgeous and rugged little town. Not only did I arrive in both a car and a coat unsuited to the Rocky Mountains, but I survived my first winter barely seeing the sun, living in a basement apartment and without a ski pass. Naturally, I welcomed the warm and impossibly green summer that finally arrived in June.

I'd written a few songs and built a small following playing covers in local restaurants, but in those days, I didn't dream of being a full-time musician. Telluride was an expensive place to live, and I had a stable, fulfilling job that paid the rent. When I walked past Elks Park and saw the songwriters performing in the Troubadour Contest, I envied their courage. Every year, 10 singer-songwriters are handpicked as finalists from thousands of submissions to compete for a coveted slot on the Main Stage, a custom Shanti guitar and the title of Telluride Troubadour. I didn't even consider it a possibility.

By the next summer, however, I was exhausted and burned out from my social work job, and I began to lean more on music to lighten up my life. Emmylou Harris played Bluegrass that year, and I nudged my way up through the crowd to watch her set. That weekend, my best friend, Emily Coleman, and I busked on Telluride's main drag, opening my guitar case for tips. I sang "Red Dirt Girl" and "If I Needed You" and secretly hoped Emmylou would walk by and hear us. She didn't.

In August of 2013, I signed up for a songwriting retreat that changed the course of my life. Not only did it inspire me to write more seriously, it plugged me into a kindred music community and revealed a path to becoming an artist that I'd never dreamed of before. I left glowing.

I knew this was a call I had to answer. I had no road map—none of us do. But I knew I had to quit my job and leave my safety net in Telluride.

Before leaving, there was one last thing I had to do: I went to the Telluride Town Park stage to say a prayer. I sat on the edge of that ramshackle wooden stage, looked out at the mountains and promised myself that the next time I walked out there, it would be to sing my own songs.

***

The following years were filled with thousands of miles on the road, making my home in an RV in parking lots and on public lands across America. My then-husband, Rous, was my cheerful co-pilot and roadie. I sang for whomever would listen and sold CDs with album covers I designed myself. One night, I played a gig in Galveston to three people. The bartender was so moved that he bought all my albums and gave us gas money. That spring, I signed with an incredible booking agent; I've never played to a three-person house since. From coffee shops to concert halls, from being completely unknown to landing in *Billboard* and *Rolling Stone*, I worked obsessively through the ups and downs to build my audience and my chops.

My career was taking off. But every year, I entered my songs into the Telluride Bluegrass Troubadour Contest, and every year I was passed over. Still, I loved going to Bluegrass as a fan. In 2017, Rous and I rolled back into town to hear my favorite artist, Brandi Carlile. She sang a new, unreleased song—"The Mother"—which stopped me in my tracks in the middle of that grassy field at dusk. Through tears I watched her bring the audience to their knees with just an acoustic guitar and a perfect song. I ached to do what she did—to make it up there and be a part of it all.

By 2019, I'd almost given up on the Troubadour contest. I'd been rejected for five years running, watching my friends and peers make it in, but

STORIES

never me. My hopes were thin and my ego a little bruised. I thought it might take another decade to earn a spot on that Bluegrass stage, and I made my peace with that. Then, an email surprised me in the middle of May. I held my breath as I scanned the list: I was a Troubadour finalist.

I took nothing for granted on that hot June day. I stood side-stage in Elks Park, fine-tuning my guitar in a blue dress and well-worn cowboy boots. I knew I had an edge in the contest: I'd been up at altitude for a month, acclimating so that I could sing effortlessly at 9,000 feet. My friends and fans made up two-thirds of the audience. I'd gotten married at the courthouse across the street and written half of my songs in these mountains. This was my home court. I felt a little guilty for how hungry I was to win. I sang high and clear, told all my best stories, brought the audience to tears and got a standing ovation.

The next day, veteran Bluegrass emcee Edee Gail announced my name and I made good on my long-ago promise. Five years after whispering my prayer, I walked out on that stage as the Troubadour winner. The weather for such a monumental day was hilariously bad—40 degrees and snowing. The Rocky Mountains like to remind you that, even in the middle of summer, winter is waiting in the wings. My friends shivered in their down jackets, faithfully cheering me on. But I don't remember feeling cold. I was levitating.

I plugged in my guitar and took a moment to look out on the mountains and the community that formed me: Telluride. The journey to that stage was hard and winding, full of doubt and wonder, and sweeter than I could have ever imagined. I had no idea that I would sign a record deal with John Prine's label two years later, or that three years later I would sing with Emmylou at the Country Music Hall of Fame. I dreamed of meeting Brandi Carlile but didn't know it would happen by surprise, backstage at the Ryman Auditorium, or that she would be so kind and warm and I would be too nervous to tell her what she meant to me.

I knew nothing of what would come after that day. I could only sense that the next chapter of my life was beginning. I whispered thanks, and raised my voice to sing.

EMILY SCOTT ROBINSON is an internationally touring artist signed to Oh Boy Records. She has four albums under her belt, and her song "Let 'Em Burn" from *American Siren* landed in the #19 slot on NPR's 100 Best Songs of 2021.

THREE POEMS

Written by ROSEMERRY WAHTOLA TROMMER

WITH ANY LUCK

Meet me in summer
when the mountains
are softened by fields
of blue lupine
and the creeks run clear
with the memory of snow.
With any luck,
we'll get lost until
we, too, begin to bloom,
until whatever is cold in us
melts and races away
with a bright and bubbling laugh.
There are days we forget
how to make a fist,
how to speak any language
but praise. Meet me
in summer when the old
high trails are open—
what else might we find
behind the crumbling
mines—some share
of ourselves we've yet
to have met—something
so spacious we never
dreamt it would fit
inside our skin.
With any luck,
it will follow us home.

WALKING UP THE PASS

A mallard swims
in the beaver pond,
the sunlight makes
green praise of its head

and for an instant
the whole world
revolves around
emerald sheen.

There is little else
that's green here,
though it is late spring—
but over 10,000 feet

the snow tends to linger.
This is a place where
the mind doesn't hesitate
to offer its attention

to the sharp scent of trees,
to the snaking trickle of snowmelt,
to the thrill of cold air
in the lungs. And in giving

itself away, the mind
becomes clearer, becomes
a shining and natural thing,
like a mallard wing, like

a tree just before leafing,
like a canyon in which
the lush green world
is just about to emerge.

STORIES

STEP BY STEP BY STEP

It's a dead end, the road.
But that is only the road.
At the end is a trail
that will lead you past
the waterfall, up through
the larkspur, waist high,
up past the turquoise
glacial lakes. And then
it ends, the trail. But
that is only the trail.
The mountains do not
end. There is the scree field
to scramble on. Clamber
up to the ridge, and then there
is over the ridge, but it is not
over, this journey. Were you
hoping that it was done?
Looking for a reason to turn
around, retrace your steps,
go home? Look. No
matter which direction
you go, you are already home.

ROSEMERRY WAHTOLA TROMMER lives with her husband and daughter in Placerville, Colorado, on the banks of the San Miguel River. She served as San Miguel County's first poet laureate (2007-2011) and as Western Slope poet laureate (2015-2017) and was a finalist for Colorado poet laureate in 2019.

STORIES

FROM "HIGH-ALTITUDE ATHLETICS"

Written by **DAVID LAVENDER**

Originally published in 1943

MY BROTHER DWIGHT was first infected with the virus, for the mountains had always been a passion with him. We had been born in the mining town of Telluride, Colorado, where the canyon of the San Miguel heads in a U-shaped basin half a mile deep. The boys of the village scrambled about the bases of the bright-colored cliffs as boys elsewhere climb trees and barns. It was an aimless zeal, however, and the idea of focusing it on a peak top never occurred to us until we had theoretically reached the age of better judgment. And then Dwight met some members of the Colorado Mountain Club.

When it developed that the club was planning a week-end assault on Mount Wilson, near Telluride, there was no restraining him. The great day arrived; we threw a pack on an old horse—we were living on the ranch then—and made a two-day ride across the hills to town.

I shall never forget the look on the hotelkeeper's face when we entered the lobby and it dawned on him that we were there to join the mountaineers. He was an odd little man, very frail and very neat, with the thin, high-domed face of an aesthete. His soft eyes peering blandly through thick spectacles made him look as though he should have been on the lecture platform of some university rather than behind the counter of a moribund hostelry. But behind it he had been since the glamour days of gold, when Telluride boasted twenty-six saloons and no church; when a quarter was the smallest coin in circulation and the conductor on the little narrow-gauge railway announced the town by bawling "To Hell You Ride." In those times champagne and caviar and terrapin had been staple items on the hotel menu; engineers' wives and mine owners' mistresses had come to its parties in Parisian gowns. Sudden death, sudden fortune, sudden poverty—all this the proprietor had seen and shared. Yet he looked at Dwight and me as though he could not believe his eyes.

"Are you going with this outfit?" he said, glancing at the climbers. We hung our heads and mumbled an admission. It was a painful moment.

As I recall it, nineteen people showed up for the trip, twelve men and seven women. Now Telluride was not as populous as it had been. The last of the great mines, the Smuggler-Union, had closed down a few years before. However, the town still remained the county seat; here and there a fresh green lawn showed that some stubborn settler was hanging on. A few fat-bellied, rusty-faced politicians wandered through the red sandstone courthouse; mountain ranchers occasionally stopped by to trade, and bewhiskered placer miners still hopefully poked about the dumps. But for the most part the stores were boarded up, and broken windows gaped in the abandoned houses. The arrival of nineteen people in a body could not escape note.

The astonished city fathers did their best. They gave us a banquet. A good one, too, with the ghosts of the hotel's old chefs rising nobly to the occasion. Instead of receiving the pieces of high-grade ore that in former days had been passed out to distinguished guests, we were treated to abundant samples of the town's last going industry—brewing. There were speeches. The beauties of the landscape were rhapsodically extolled by men whose axes and dredges and dynamite had done their best to destroy that beauty. The old phrase "Switzerland of America"—every mountain sector of the West calls itself that—was trotted out and dusted off by half-a-dozen willing throats.

Warmed by their own voices and their own beer, the hosts began having a wonderful time. Then, just as the party was taking on the faint blush of former celebrations, the climbers all stood up and went to bed. They were leaving for the assault at four o'clock the next morning and they wanted to leave fresh. Incomprehensibility worse confounded! If the dismayed city fathers needed further evidence of idiocy, here it was.

Four o'clock the next morning was cheerless. Dawn had not yet come, and no stars were visible in the sodden sky. However, weather is one of the accepted hazards of climbing. We piled into cars and away we went along the narrow, breath-taking dirt road that skirts the vast upper gorges of the San Miguel. Eventually, after passing through the huddle of huts which is Ophir and skidding wildly along the greasy branch road that leads to Dunton, we reached a high, alpine vale known as Dunton Meadows. Here we left the cars and set out afoot. It was daylight now, but Mount Wilson was not to be seen. Clouds lay on the treetops.

* * *

Our leaders ran the gamut on that Wilson climb. Trail finding was the worst. At lower elevations we encountered mazes of timber falls and impenetrable thickets of underbrush. We struggled through what seemed like miles of scree and talus, steep slopes of shattered slide rock that have fallen from the cliffs and roll backward under you with every step you take. Rain drenched us, and as we climbed higher we were presented with the odd spectacle of snow going straight up instead of down.

This phenomenon was occasioned by the wind whipping through the basin below. When it met the towering ridge along whose knife-edged summit we were worming our way it was deflected upward with its burden of sleet. The effect, as we crouched there in our lonely miasma of mist, was indescribably weird. It was also cold. I had no gloves, but for some reason I had slipped an extra pair of woolen socks in my pocket. I put these on my hands. The luxury was wonderful—until I noticed, though I tried hard not to, that one of the ladies of the party was also gloveless. I surrendered my socks. Never have I enjoyed so rich a feeling of chivalry or suffered so from frozen fingers.

* * *

When we finally staggered on to the fog-shrouded summit it was 6:00 p.m. We had no desire to wolf out the night on the mountaintop, yet we knew that fatalities might well repay any attempt by nineteen tired people to descend in pitch-darkness the exposed cliffs we had climbed. Brows knit, the board of strategy went into a huddle. It was decided to select a much longer but safer route to the sheltering timber some three thousand feet below. Westward, long snow slopes dropped into a basin—Killpacker Basin, some disgusted packer had named it long ago. After reaching its bottom, rounding its southern arm, and then doubling back through the spruce forests, we could, we hoped, regain our cars without breaking our necks.

* * *

Toward dawn we located the cars, returned to Telluride, and collapsed into bed. My first organized climb was over.

    The next evening I came down to the hotel lobby, ravenous and creaking in every joint. The proprietor asked, with some maliciousness, I thought, "Well, did you like it?"

DAVID LAVENDER [1910-2003] grew up near Telluride, steeped in the ranching and mountaineering cultures of the early 20th century. He documented this era as a historian and short-story writer, becoming one of the foremost chroniclers of the American West. This selection is excerpted from his acclaimed 1943 book *One Man's West*.

INDEX

INDEX

1914 flood 10, 39
1976 drug bust 33
221 South Oak 16
Abbey, Edward 24, 60
Ah Haa School for the Arts 52, 61
Allred's 16
Alpine lakes 41
Alpino Vino 16, 47
Alta Lakes 8, 19, 41
Alternating-current electricity 32
Avalanche dogs 36
Backus, Harriet Fish 9
Ballard Mountain 46
Basecamp 550 53
Beaver 33
Between the Covers 7, 18, 75
Bivvi Hostel Telluride 9
Black bear 33
Black Iron Bowl 47
Blue Lake 41
Blue Lakes 41
Blues & Brews Festival 20
Boling, Ashley 19
Bon Vivant 17
Bonneau, Ryan 21
Breakfast burrito 8
Bridal Veil Backcountry Ski Camp 53
Bridal Veil Falls 8, 41
Brown Dog Pizza 17
Butcher & The Baker, The 8, 16
Camp V 53
Caravan 17
Carter, Tara 21
Cassidy, Butch 10, 34
Chair Nine 47
Chesonis, Daiva 74
Coffee Cowboy 47
Columbia 10, 26
Columbine Lake 41
Cornet Creek Falls 46
Cosmopolitan 17
Crossbow Leather 18
Depot, The 31
Dunton Hot Springs 18, 53
Dunton Town House 9
Elk 26, 33
Esquivel, Maria "Lupita" 68
Fig, The 19
First Thursday Art Walk 20
Fleck, Béla 9, 10
Floradora Saloon 17
Flowers By Ella 18
Free Box, The 27
Galloping Goose, The 11, 37
Ghosts 24
Gold King Mine 32
Gondola, The 8, 74
Goodtimes, Art 58
Gorrono Ranch 16
Grateful Dead, The 36
Green, Kathy 60
Hardrock 100 26
Haugen, Lars 40
Heidger, Tom 21
History 10, 19, 29, 39
Hope Lake 41
Imogene Pass Run 64
Island Lake 41
Issenberg, Lisa 63
Jagged Edge Mountain Gear 18
Jud Wiebe Trail 19
Kearney, Harry 66
Kenworthy, Gus 21
Klein, Josh 21
KOTO 8
Kozak, Mark 21
La Cocina de Luz 17
La Marmotte 17
Last Dollar Ski Hut 53
Lauterbach, Heidi 21
Lavender, David 88
Longbaugh, Harry 34
Lumière with Inspirato 9
Madeline Hotel & Residencies 9
Martin, Art 30
Mill Creek bike trails 46
MiXX Projects + Atelier 52
Mushroom Festival 20, 58
Nabokov, Vladimir 27
National, The 8, 16

New Sheridan Chop House 16
New Sheridan Hotel 9, 10, 30, 39
New Sheridan Parlor 9, 17
Nothing Festival, The 35
Nugget Theatre 31, 52
Oak 16, 47
Observatory at Alta Lakes, The 41, 53
Original Thinkers Festival 20
Orvis Hot Springs 19
Osgood, Mason 21
Over the Moon 18
Peaks Resort & Spa 9
Petite Maison 17
Rebolledo Léon, Ximena 21
Robinson, Emily Scott 9, 80
Rustico 17
Sadowsky, Dan 9
San Juan Hut System 53
San Miguel Basin Rodeo 20
San Miguel County Courthouse 31
See Forever 47
Shaunette, Geneva 71
Sheridan Opera House 8, 52
Siam 17
Silver Bell, The 24
Ski history 29
Skoloda, Jeff 21

Slate Gray Gallery 52
Slate, The 7, 38
Smuggler Union 17
Sneffels Highline Trail 19, 25
Spindler, Joanna 21
Steen, Matt 65
Straight Creek Journal, The 33
Stronghouse 17
Talking Gourds 20, 58
Telluride Adaptive Sports Program 21
Telluride AIDS Benefit Fashion Show 20
Telluride Angler 18
Telluride Arts 52
Telluride Bike Path 46
Telluride Bluegrass Festival 7, 9, 20, 80
Telluride Bottle Works 18
Telluride Brewing Company 17
Telluride Film Festival 7, 20, 52
Telluride Gay Ski Week 20
Telluride Hiking Guide 46
Telluride Historical Museum 8, 24, 31
Telluride Historical Museum 24, 31
Telluride Jazz Festival 10, 20
Telluride Magazine 8
Telluride Mountain Guides 19

Telluride Music Co. 18
Telluride Nordic Association 19
Telluride Outfitters 19
Telluride Outside 19
Telluride Ski & Golf Club 19
Telluride Ski Resort 11, 19, 29
Telluride Toggery 7, 18, 33
Telluride Transfer Warehouse 52, 71
Telluride Truffle 18
Telluride Via Ferrata 46, 61
There 8, 17
Timber Room 17
Timberline Ace Hardware 18
Tomboy Bride 9
Town Hall 31, 38
Town Park 8, 21, 81
Trommer, Rosemerry Wahtola 84
Trout Lake 41, 46
True Grit 9
Trujillo, Rick 64
Ute tribe 8, 10, 39
Wagner Custom Skis 18
Watenpaugh, Jane 69
Wildflowers 25, 41, 46
Williams, Roger Neville 33
YX Factor, The 9
Zoline, Joseph T. 30

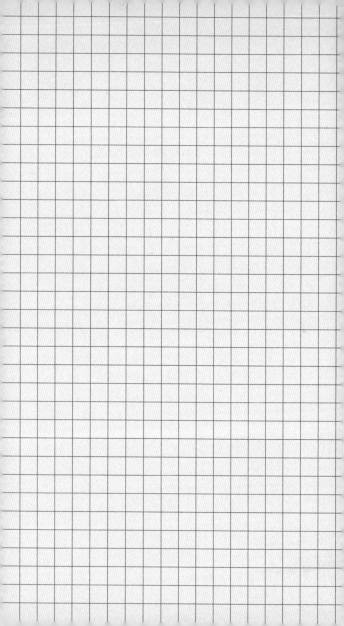